devorah major

word time

poems

CITY LIGHTS BOOKS
SAN FRANCISCO

word time

Cover design by Jeff Mellin
Text design by Patrick Barber

Library of Congress Cataloging-in-Publication Data

Names: Major, Devorah, 1952– author.
Title: Word time / by Devorah Major.
Other titles: Word time (Compilation)
Description: San Francisco, CA : City Lights Books, 2025.
Identifiers: LCCN 2025022363 (print) | LCCN 2025022364 (ebook) | ISBN 9780872869417 (paperback) | ISBN 9780872869424 (epub)
Subjects: LCGFT: Poetry.
Classification: LCC PS3563.A3915 W67 2025 (print) | LCC PS3563.A3915 (ebook) | DDC 811/.54—dc23/eng/20250602
LC record available at https://lccn.loc.gov/2025022363
LC ebook record available at https://lccn.loc.gov/2025022364

City Lights Books are published at the City Lights Bookstore
261 Columbus Avenue, San Francisco, CA 94133
citylights.com

Praise for devorah major and *word time*

"Songful poems which are incantatory origin stories, which as only sublime poetry can do, remake us, make us see ourselves—*all* of us—anew. By way of the personal in the historical, the historical in the personal, as well as in cosmic contexts. With the lexicon and linguistics of love. Which is what happens over and over again when you read and reread *word time*, major's wonderful new collection."
—**Everett Hoagland**, author of *The Music: New & Selected Poems 1973–2023*

"devorah major has been an enduring voice in the Bay Area literary scene for many years, and *word time* is her strongest and most powerful work to date. Broken into title sections of particles of speech, *word time* journeys back to the 'demon ship,' when the shackle and the splitting of the tongue began her ancestral trauma of the physical and psychological subjugation. The rupture and loss of major's African lineage, once rich with ancient lore, cultural wisdom, art and spirituality, is the treasure she seeks to reclaim in the psychic ruins of her people. Each poem, in a sense, is both, invocation and exorcism, a painful confrontation with both perpetrators and victims of the historic past to the present day. It is a rite of healing and reconciliation, through the writing process of what Toni Morrison called 'rememory.' We, as readers, can't help but be swept by the gravitational pull of her journey of love and loss, because it ultimately connects all of our convergences, across all oceans and borders, whether as descendants of slaves, indentured servants, immigrants, migrants, wayfinders, or colonial settlers."
—**Genny Lim**, San Francisco Poet Laureate

"In a world filled with the obtuse variety of raucous soundwaves plaguing our every minute, major leads us into an ease-like force field of stream-driven poetry; a revival of timelessness; Oshun at peace in a meditative state of understanding, acceptance & pleasure."
—**mimi tempestt**, author of *the delicacy of embracing spirals*

"devorah major writes knowing only language can hold us together. Her poems are a bridge over troubled waters. There is anger and sadness in this collection as major acknowledges the city morning blues. History is a witness to 'the theft' of her ancestors. *word time* brings the juju of salvation. major writes: *time does not move / it is the earth that shakes / the sky that rushes / we who surge.* This book contains the language of memories and the American truth. major's work echoes Coltrane's *A Love Supreme.* There is a spiritual honesty here that underscores her skill as a poet."
—**E. Ethelbert Miller**, author of *the little book of e*

"Every line in devorah major's *word time* ignites the page. A book-length scat that transforms words into a new instrument, this collection is a 'slap snap/siren whirl/holler/electric zip' all at once. The poems deliver spectacular images that convey the beauty and the horror of 'undeniable american truths,' and provide an antidote to the 'enslaved curriculum.' Each line, each poem title, delivers a resounding beat and tempo that reveal the bounty that major's body of work, and this newest book in particular, hold. devorah major, San Francisco's third Poet Laureate, continues to write witness and resistance, in her full power, with the keenest eye and an exacting pen."
—**Leticia Hernández-Linares**, author of *Mucha Muchacha, Too Much Girl*

contents

word time

word time

how old is your language
he asks and pauses
for answers that will not
come to the tongue

my language of memories
is buried in bone marrow
spilling out in blood
rich with copper
salt and ancestor breath

my language of touch was
inherited from the first ones
who tasted green, swallowed night
and learned by stroke
and knead to know each other

my language of dance
choreographed on waves
and undulant meadow grasses
now rests in lamp-lit shadows

and my language of speech
is words welded and wielded
round the globe

a language of jazz and goobers
okra and okay opening
the wow of africa

while hindi lies with norse
and german is a bedfellow of latin

a trade language english
smelted by a people committed
to war and domination

my language bends and recreates itself
claims a lineage measured
across light years of knowing
forgetting and learning once
again

nouns

oshun's cloth

if oshun is weaver
then what are any of us
but finely colored fibers
the threads
the cloth
and the song
from her loom

creation paradox

we hold the great-great
grandparents of our ancestors'
grandparents
in our bloodstreams
in our guts
in our hearts
thousands of years
rest inside our souls

in those years lives the record
of our beginning
it is the sweetest marrow
in our spine
the cleanest shine in our eyes
the open side of our laughter
you can read it in the lines
on the soles of our feet

when we retell the stories
of where we came from
we draw back tree branches
to find hidden fruits which we savor
pointed thorns which make us bleed
the yesterdays that led to here
the heres that lead to tomorrow

when we go back to the beginning
we find the stars thousands of years
thousands and thousands of years

in the beginning there was a time

we all say
when we were not

after that time
we became

we were created
we were molded
we were spewed out
we were sung into
until we learned
how to make
what to form
why to sing

but once
long ago
in the beginning
there was only one
and from the one
others were born
and out of those many

came us
that is the story
we all tell

but
before that beginning
before the in the beginning
beginning when we were born
there must have been another beginning

before the spider crafting web
laying sixteen eggs

before the mountain birthing lovers
birthing children

before the sky settling low
to mate with earth

before light
before darkness
before breath even

there must have been
another beginning

a beginning that lives
in a place we call
unknowable
yet is braided
into our genealogies

and it is said
that it is in this beginning
the beginning before our beginning
it is there that you must go
if you want to find the faces of god

thousands of years
thousands and thousands of years
rest inside
our souls

saltwater crossings

did our waters of salt breathe
as we birthed our young
did we swim those laughing waves
before the wrenching
before the tearing
before the theft

did we harvest our ocean's bounty
fish to feed our families
and with thankfulness did we
offer her fresh flower songs
that were swallowed by her crests
we did do we did do

did we cleanse our wounds
in her seas and discover our dreams
inside those silver midnight waves

did we listen to the ancestors' guidance
as the surf met the sand

did we know and relish
the waters of salt
before their arrivals
before our crossings
we did do we did do

before we were packed
into strange ship hulls
chained naked and trapped
in an evil we had never imagined

we did not know these waters as venom
we learned their sting as they were
poured in buckets over
our bruised and torn bodies
to wash away the stench of
blood, feces, and razor tears

its salt bite was bitter
as our homes turned
to memory
to myth
and then
were forgotten

all was salt and moan
soaking through our skin
to live forever
in the marrow of our bones

we did not see the stars change
did not know when
the moon was hungry and fierce
or full and satiated

but we knew salt

we ate its curses
we savored its healing
we learned its lessons
and we survived

island woman speaks of tongues

they took my words
all of them not knowing
that in my home I spoke
many languages
not only to family
traders and voyagers
but to hawk and monkey
sandpiper and dolphin

they took my tongue
gripped my throat tightly
and commanded me
to use only their words
yes sir madam
limited ideas
that did not tell
of spirit or legacy

we will not speak of the bakra who
as we tossed in the belly
of their demon ship
tore into me like a spear
chasing the neck of a lion
spilling my blood
yet leaving inside
the seedling of a son

my son whom i taught all
my remembered languages
until he understood
wind and star and smoothed
his freedom road whistling
the birds to quiet their song
as he passed by sending
a raven to my window
to let me know
he was now a man
unfettered

some call me
obeah woman
ask me to make juju
so they could become invisible
so all the bakra would dry up and die
so we could return home

but now i only know of healing song
and the gift of animal languages
and learned words
the invaders, rapists and slavers
would not teach me
like survive
struggle
surmount

prepositions

in my now

the past hovers in front of my eyes
beacons of warning flash
oases of pleasure reflect
as its sepia tones fade

the future at my back is yet unseen
but its heat blisters my skin
its barbs tear at my clothes
and its winds thrust me forward

city scat

we come to this city
of concrete, brick
steel and toil

country people
knowing the earth

seafaring people
reading the tides

gambling people
holding jokers and spades

we come to this city

hard laughin'
weep sob wailin'
prayin' celebratin' people
bendin' and sweatin'

we come to
this hiss crack
slap snap
siren whirl
holler

electric zip
and burn
city

rounding
bustling corners
banging our heads
against destiny
and crumbling
brick walls of confusion

we come to this city
that can cage us
enrage us
deny us
revile us
turn us
from friends and family
into prey and predator

we live in this city
this hip howl
she bop
da he bop
da we bop
bang clang
swinging city

we reclaim
all of our neighbors
in the hood who
keep our hearts beating
with the rhythms of drums

we come to this city
and we name it ours

a little night music

laugh
chat
yell
tire screech
dog barks
a contrapuntal chorus
riding the night air

some evenings
a concert of gunfire
glass breaking sirens
assault trembling windows

kaleidoscopic flashes
color dark breezes
at the crossroads

morning blues

swallowing blue from a flattened sky
as the bridge's sculpted silver arc
rises above the ripple reflecting bay

car radio coughs details
police executions of
black and brown men
their crime far beyond skin color

one man ran towards the light
asserting he would not be
murdered in the dark

yelling out that
he wanted them to
see him when they killed him

and they did

this evening on 8th and wood

he is pleading
for the other man to see

we are brothers he says
you and me me and you

you were always
there for me to lean on
me there for you always

I love you man I love you
again and again releasing words
without inhalation

just a giving

soul bound to soul
with time and experience
his voice rides urgency

no one wants to lose anyone tonight
I don't want to lose anyone
you don't want to lose anyone
no one has to lose anyone

the voice ebb and flow quiets
as the blade edge
on which the words teetered
transforms into steam
and they are breathing together

I cannot see either one
an energy of youth but
no knowing of what has made
one rise up against the other

how they occupy space

did I hear right
a new voice raspy and thin
I don't want to get shot
and quiet again
quiet and still

undeniable american truths

the elders were slain
and the tears flowed
they poured out of our eyes
down cracked sidewalks
and trickled into the gutters
where they traveled with refuse
into the nation's rivers and oceans

the children were murdered
and the tears flowed
they poured out of our eyes
they fell on hard concrete
and were swallowed in gutters
where they were washed with waste
into the nation's streams and bays

more locks were bought
and of course
more guns

and the tears flowed
onto the flat gray sidewalks
and seeped into gutters
where they slid with the litter
into the nation's lakes and oceans
as people beat their chests

pulled out their hair
buried their dead

and finally newspeak pundits
discovered that
this is indeed who
we americans are

we murder our elders
we murder our children
we murder people at prayer
at music concerts
at dance clubs
at schools
at grocery stores
at home
we murder
and then we lower flags to half-mast
and we speak of "thoughts and prayers"

we mouth condolences
to the families and loved ones
flowers are stacked
stuffed animals are propped
balloons flown
ribbons tied at massacre sites
candlelit vigils are held in dark shadows

and we cry
and we watch our tears
fall on concrete
and get fed into sewers
as we stand as memorial statues
frozen in a pivotal moment of war
and do
nothing

given what is taken

it may be insane to remain
sane in these times
as settlers' rifles
aimed and cocked

at you and your young
indicate signs displayed
everywhere insisting on subservience

news reports
of your worthlessness
are pounded into
blood-soaked sidewalks

making it easy and
altogether sane
given what is taken

to go mad
to lose your footing
to slip into tunnels painted
with screeches of abuse

to feel the noose
slide down the neck
cinching a stranglehold on reason

the iron truncheon aimed
at the softer parts of your nature
almost forces you to reform
under the mask of insanity

eyes become bulbous or
turn to slits
cut into parchment paper

face bones soften
and re-sculpt themselves
sharpened into angled blades

the streets will make you mad
if you let them
and even if you don't

the crazed roller coaster
tram will carry you to its crest
without you having to buy a ticket

you will be freefalling through space
coming closer to but never close enough
to hit the concrete concourse below

and with your fists of sweated fury
your brain and heart will
given what has been taken
very sanely become altogether mad

interjections

lynch defined

2023 the first full year after lynching was declared a federal crime

lynch fist panic punches
lynch steel-toed boot barrage
lynch truncheon beating
lynch rope hell hang
lynch river rogue drown
lynch bullet eviscerate
lynch cage shackled
lynch lynch lynch

lynched blacks standing tall
lynched blacks writhing on the ground
lynched blacks sitting in a car
lynched blacks pressed against a wall
lynched blacks swinging in a cell
lynched blacks dangling from a pole
lynched blacks crying for their mother
lynched blacks innocent of crime
cut down again and still again

engrave their names on museum plaques
admit them into the growing club
of over four centuries
of government sanctioned
murder

and then in unity rise up
in their honor
with more than voices
placards and feet

king thoughts

1.

"king me"
my brother said
then bored by
the simplicity of checkers
he tried to teach me chess

"don't worry about the king
the queen has all the power"

but he soon tired
of my unwillingness
to sacrifice the pawns
and use my knights effectively

2.

king size beds are good to play in but
hard to find affordable sheets to cover

3.

king size sodas good to share
in a family of six
with ample dental benefits
and no predilection towards diabetes

4.

king tut was a boy
who followed
the directions of self-serving
men who wanted to be
but never truly were
kings

5.

king kong, a tragic primate
of questionable ancestry born
from the brain of a man
who hated and feared black
but acknowledged a king size heart
inside that gorilla frame
that could be killed
but not controlled

6.

a king for children the elephant babar
lives well in understated colors and tightly
drawn doodles by heavily taxing
his subjects who he rules with an ivory tusk

7.

king henry the 8th was a murderer
of women impotent in his madness
and king leopold of belgium

a despot taking limbs and lives of congolese
who before leopold ruled
breathed song with their mornings
instead of axe, blood and severed arms

8.

the king of spades is always trumped by an ace
and can be easily beguiled by the queen of hearts
if she knows when and how to play her cards

9.

the king of the road
has never been the king of rock
who must concede his title
to the king of soul who gave him
a corner on the platform
already shared
with the king of blues

9 a.

(there is no king of jazz
anarchy and democracy
rule improvisation
around chord changes)

10.

and as for martin luther
he was no king

a seer for some
prophet for others
a man whose heart contained the world
but he wore no crown

no crown of thorns
no crown of gold
only a dream painted
in multitudes of colors
stitched with prayers
which were always a call to action

II.

"king me,"
my brother said
and I placed a rounded checker
black against black
upon his piece

"king me," he said

and I did
again
and again

enslaved curriculum

Florida's academic standards of 2023 Social Studies curriculum will now include lessons on how "slaves developed skills" that could be used for "personal benefit."

quiet your yelling
child what they say is true

many a skill of survival
that was of personal benefit was
learned while we were enslaved

this was told to me by my grandmother
as it was told to her by her grandmother
as I am now telling it to you

we learned how to doctor flesh
lacerated by horse whip lashings
so that it could heal without infection
before it turned to thick knotted scars

we learned how to engrave our babies' skin
so that if they were torn from our bosoms
and we found them again

even if they were all the way grown
we would know by their markings
this one was our own

we learned how to sing
coded songs steering runaways
towards guiding stars and freedom trails

and how to take a glass the master broke
and grind it small enough to hide in a
sweet rice pudding so that his gut would
drip blood until his life breath vanished
leaving only the malevolence of his wretched soul

remember child
we brought prayer from Africa
already knew how to farm
harvest and cook
fashion a home
weave and dye cloth
work iron and heal sickness

we brought all that with us

but we learned of things
learned of ways
we never imagined
or needed to know

we learned how to keep Africa veiled inside
no matter how they tried to
burn her memory out with their iron crosses
and endless beatings

we stitched Africa in the quilts we made
and hung on our walls and across our beds

we kept it in the ways
we braided and wrapped our hair

the ways we danced our pain and joy
sang out our hopes and lessons

we learned that we could tune their language
until it became ours holding on
to African time and tone

and despite it all we learned
how to keep on loving each other
in all our shades and hues

we learned how some could
fear history and deny truth
and we learned the color of evil
was not the color of us

so when they ask what we learned
when enslaved that was a benefit
in this stolen hate-filled land

you sit up tall
raise your hand
and let that teacher know
what we truly learned
how we taught each other
those truths

how we're still learning
still teaching
and won't ever stop

untitled quilts

there's this thing some folks have
about names and namin'

I got so many names floating around
the one I was born with

the ones my two husbands give to me
the one that collecting jewish man gave

sayin' it would be a shield between me and strangers
tho' it turned out to be more of a flag far as I could see

and then too there was how folks was always
asking me to name my pieces*

like they was chirrens or something
but they all come from the same place

and sooner or later they all
end up at the same destination

though they be taking different directions as they grow
so why they need different names/any names

truth be said they all be my conversations with god
sometimes about living and sometimes crossin' over

sometimes about where i lay my head to sleep
or sometimes where I used to call home

and more times than not
scripture is wrapped in there too

even though I don't most times write it out
only when I want to make sure

folk know the story that led me to the pattern
the way I shape silent prayers in colors

make them fit, the why of it all
but most times they just prayers and conversation

me openin' up and singin' to my god in my way
with my needles and scraps of cloth and colored
    threads

but there's this thing people got about namin' things
a whole lot of sin come from namin' something wrong

so my pieces they all have something to do with god
and they untitled like me and god's conversations with
    each other

**A piece becomes a quilt after it has a back and is filled and bordered.*

Renowned Arkansas raised and California transplanted (African) American quilter Effie Mae Howard had her professional name changed to Rosie Lee Tompkins when she began to get famous for her pieces.

lining up

get in line
where's the line
conga line?
electric slide
line dance line
smooth across the floor

write a line
"line, please"
make a line
rhyme the line
not this time

hold the line
tight now
acknowledge the tearful first line
parade to the brass filled second line
dancing back from the graveyards of memory
of the lost and forgotten
of the martyred and murdered
in front of police lines
military lines
death lines

don't toe the line
slip below that line

forget about the borderline
this land knows no lines
is owned by itself
unceded by the indigenous
caretakers who knew no lines
between sea and mountain
desert and valley
except the fault lines
hidden beneath earth's mantle
causing the land to rumble and crack

don't cross the line
be the line
the family line
the ancestral line
hold it tight
push it forward

do not ignore confederate lines
drawn in devotion to an endless war
composed of thick armed lines
white on one side
the rainbow's promise on the other
cut that line

move to the front of the line

battle lines formed
by those who love humanity
cherish our colors
celebrate all bloodlines
relish all the lines we share and cross

hold the line against those
who spew hate and ignorance
spout it like skunk weed fouling the air

our future lines are
determined by our strength
not jive lines trying
to catch someone on the sidelines
not phone lines full of static
and weak connections

but by freedom full lifelines
existing without flags or doctrine
inside drumlines beating out
sustaining rhythms
to our soulful song lines

downpressors

"Woe to the downpressors:
They'll eat the bread of sorrow!"

BOB MARLEY

you walked on our bones for centuries
turned them to sand
poured into sandboxes
for your children to build sandcastles

and when the sand became translucent
filled with the sunlight
burning your eyes
you found more to sacrifice

sent vultures to strip away our skins
and built ladders formed
from our ribs, limbs and skulls
on which you climbed
to get a better view of the lands
you planned to conquer

and now we rise
joined by
some of your children
and grandchildren
who have eaten of shame
and refuse to travel

on the rails you laid
with our bones

and each of you
who blocks our path
tries to press us back
will be blinded by our brilliance
blinded
blinded
blinded by our brilliance

war observed

1.

as death melts into the earth
the living are dressed
with the spirits of their dead
pressed into heavy coats
and thick solid shoes

some men bend but do not fall
with the buildings around them

2.

there are moments
when all tears are spent
all howls quieted
and only the music of bombardment
and crumbling houses can be heard

is death complicated
or simply final

3.

grandmother now
she sits in a corner

of a room of refuge
one arm
gone
one leg
crushed
one husband
buried
one home
demolished

she does not name
those responsible

her truth is that
those who shoot
who bomb
who kill
do not fear god
or seek justice
only twisted revenge

her lips are welded
eyes neither embracing nor
turning from the camera

4.

do not ask
the widow who
the child how
the mother why
or if there is value to
the dying
for dominion
for capital
for flags
that wave above graveyards

5.

only soldiers can stop it
soldiers cannot refuse to die
but they can refuse to kill

6.

the solution lives
in tears carried in
smoke filled wind
above the silences
that follow bombs collisions

7.

his lens sees only tragedy
the crumbled kitchen
the hollowed bedroom
the little girl
the baby
the mother
the son
the eyes forever frozen into discs
like the camera's lens
frigid with the ice of terror

he puts the camera down
finds water for this one
lifts the body of that one
seeks another way to
hold back the war's tide

childhoods remembered

do you remember holding
your small child hand up to
your father's large comforting hand
amazed at its size compared
to your vine thin fingers

do you remember making
fingers and palms
into church and steeple
and then opening to see all the people

do you remember drawing
eyes and mouths on fingers
creating silly finger people

thumb folded around
pointer finger making a mouth
opening and closing

silly games of childhood
laughter crawling down our bodies
dissolving in the air
and reappearing
as a tickle giggle
finger wiggle

remember

not wanting to be one of the missing
or one of the unable to be identified killed
the little girl wrote on the inside of her
heart shaped palm between heart
and lifelines in neat Arabic script
"if my hand survived
this is my name" before she was slain

these children do not have
numbers burned into their arms
but many have written their own
names statements and identification numbers

pants legs rolled up reveal
the brothers inscribed legs reading
Ahmad Nateel
Jowan Nateel
Rebhan Nateel

did the oldest write it for his younger brothers
or were they perhaps written by a trembling mother
or a father writing while damming his own tears

now they lie next to each other
softly browned saplings chopped down
before they could bear fruit

the whole family it seems
assassinated in what their killers
call a cleansing
a mowing of grass
a righteous final solution

are you old enough to remember being a child
old enough to remember growing up
maybe even remember becoming old

they are not
their dead bodies
reflect the memories they will never have

one child has written on her arm
"no I will not die"

does she still live

how hate was born

perhaps you wonder
how hate was born.

some say it has always been
part of the air we breathe
but this is not true

the first ones wove the cord
of our continuum
bubbling with truth
born with our ancestors' echo

one humanity with many hues
one people with many songs
one planet with infinite fruits to be shared

but somehow that cord frayed
and some began to let go
when they began to fear each other
began to fear those who pulled away
those who crafted different ways
those who sang other notes
beat out dissimilar rhythms
who savored other spices

people began to fear
losing what they held
began to fear not having enough
and pushed aside the others
to get more
ever more

forgetting the lessons of sharing
betraying the truth
of the one human family

they began to smelt hate
on fear's blade
thicken hate with fear's tar
etch hate in fear's acid

they began to hate
what they feared
who they feared
covered the sludge
of hate around their fear
so they could not see fear
so they could not hear fear
as long as they kept the hate
viscous, viral, and virulent

they did not seek understanding
sought only to scorn, to reject

to spurn, to demean
to destroy with their poisoned fruit of hate

and this is how and where hate now flourishes
like blind white termites eating away
at supporting beams of humanity's shelters

all fear does not gestate hate
but hate is always born of fear

hate's history is long and violent
but if we all can learn again to sing together
one humanity with many hues
one people with many songs
one planet with infinite fruits to be shared
hate will have little to feed upon

the bounty of age

slowing down with the pull of piled years
patterns emerge that eluded us before

slowing lets us see love's ebbs and flows
like gulls moving as winged clouds
around the beach to part as if cleaved
then reunite soaring ever higher into the sky

a tale of capitulation and resistance is told
in the randomness of kelp piles and wisps

the bounty of aging is
that even as one's eyes weaken
sight becomes more keen

pronouns

poetry lovers

you ask
do poetry lovers
make love

do the metaphors awaken
do the verbs excite
do the ideas caress

is there heavy breathing
in the subject matter
moans in
the line breaks
deep penetration
in the subtext

is there sweat
and scent
and laughter

it's all about
word choice
and exchange

affection
without affectation

acceptance
without demands

questions that can remain
unanswered
answers that have
open endings

or no ending at all

just satisfaction
in touching
and being touched
in a heartfelt way

unspoken love

lightly we step on ice
that may be far too thin

or perhaps it is the hour
too early or too late

the sky veiled by clouds
threatens rivers of rain

even as spring hints
a future flower song

seaside walks and you

for Everett

on your meandering
eventide walks
i imagine you
inhale the sea

its salt and cloud reflections
the birds that swoop to catch
and swallow their prey

the kelp, sand and shells
ship memories of slavers' hulls
filled with africa's bounty

sunsets colored of
blood and gold
the music of its waves

as splash and chortles
as cymbal and bells
as rumble and croon

you taste its years
which measured against yours
keep you young yet

agile in mind and spirit
if not always in bone and sinew
heart like seaside
rhythms murmur and rock

decades of living next to
its lessons have sharpened
your knowing and deepened
your spirit and bound you

in some ancient way to your kin
stolen from other ocean shores
where salt also filled the air

and the ocean's song
caroled into the evening's darkness

lived in beaded gourds
and skin stretched drums
that you might hear intoned

in your sunrise dreams
and lovingly embed
in your smoothly crafted poems

measured time

before belief there was
only a now
that was eternal

then when we
conceived our gods
created our universe
there became a time before

now gone

and a time after
now here

and a time yet to be
beyond belief

listening to *a love supreme*

coltrane calls
for a love supreme
wails a prayer for us

to become a chorus

of a love that can never become hate
a love that will never fade, sputter, die
a love that has no price tags
a love without asterisk
a love that is not inconvenient
heavy, crude, cliché
a love not found in a bubblegum love song
or a steamy romance novel
a love without metaphor
because it is not like or as anything
except itself

a love that at its root
is pure
as prayer
as song
as gift

a love supreme

conjunctions

error in time 2

Time a traveler   melting
in eternity
(the mind coming and going)
FERLINGHETTI, *Back Roads to Far Places*

time exists
only as a contract
we keep or break
a memory we smell or
forget a terror
we confront or duck
a bridge we blow up
or build

time does not move
it is the earth that shakes
the sky that rushes
we who surge

time does not change
the world changes as we
nourish or devour
the life around us

not in time
not on time
not despite time

but always
in the moments
named now

rise

we bow with respect
kneel in homage
give thanks to our ancestors

and then we rise

we bend in harsh storms
we stumble and fall
pull each other back up
broken at times
but we heal

and then we rise

they stuff our mouths with their fear
twist our children with their venom
deny our history
breaking all mirrors
which reflect our true selves

but we
wash our mouths
with flowing river water

cleanse our eyes
with gentle spring rains

take our children to the sea
and unwind their limbs

as we tell them the stories
of how we've survived
of how we carry
our ancestors' breath
inside our mouths

we teach our children
who we have been
and who they are
and why we must
learn to climb mountains
with sturdy ropes
and enduring faith

of why we must
climb closer and closer
to the sun
so that we
like it
will rise
cut through fog
melt thick layered ice
and watch our crops grow

how to avoid extinction

be wide and malleable
wing and sledgehammer
root and claw

know when and how to burrow
create cave or foxhole
find cavern or gulch

hold onto ancestor stories
the birthing
growing
dying
rebirth

sew tone rhyme
rhythm stories
into your skin
thread them between teeth
eat them as sacred fruit

and live as they live
forever

who shall inherit the earth

in amharic
i once heard
the correct translation
was not the meek
broken
crushed
humiliated
low
who would inherit the earth
but the gentle

and we are

inheriting
these streets
even as we sleep on them
and are swept up only to return

sharp the edges of so many of our lives
fierce with hunger and pain

so much disillusionment
and so very few triumphs

even as the rulers
squeeze tighter

cutting short our breath
hobbling our steps

harnessed together we will
inherit the earth

such as it is

sad with violence and pestilence
the air clotted and gray
islands covered with an
ever rising sea churning
churning

still it is becoming ours

even as they wage
their gruesome wars

killing and selling
buying and exporting death

advertising the price for each kill
factored into the decision
to research develop manufacture
and buy the newest weapon
to kill more quickly
more anonymously

even in the face of this hegemony of arms
every side buys from every side
every side sells to every side

even the pawns choose their weapons
aim and fire and die

still, we gentle are joining
together more and more tightly
inheriting the earth
from these others who want
only to have
to hold
to own
to control
as if they were hurricane and sun
arrogant in their perceived power

not understanding that
all of it will explode
or else disintegrate

and they will be left with
misshapen impotent stories
of the times that used to be

while we will remain
remembering our many
losses along the way

still wounded and reeling
we gentle will
inherit the earth

pull out our seed stock
and begin to plant anew

an eternity of life

we are
the dust of stars
and have travelled far
to come to this place

and live the story of humans
where our blood
tells tales of our journeys
around the universe

remembered stories
of woven helixes forming
the marrow of our bones
and offering our ancestors
the gift of our survival

our breath
is the substance of stars
that burned for eons
exploding and imploding
birthing and rebirthing life

we are this place

we are this place
the clay and salt of it
the river and sand of it

fingers rise from desert dunes
faces emerge from cresting waves
bodies unfold like tropical blossoms
flush with the odors of honey and decay

we are the forests we fell
the mountains we devour
the lands we poison
our bodies are
the seed and ash of this place

we are not merely the caretakers of this place
we are this place, this place of gold and silt

and what will we do with this gift and debt
where in prayer is the space for truth
when amidst these interminable wars
is the table of compassion set

even in our worm selves as we turn and spit
fertilizing the future with our waste
we are so much more than we imagine

we are spirit resilient
rock unforgiving
wind eternal

let us move now
from the storms of hate and fear
and cleanse this place that is us

sacrifice nothing but our arrogance
and the need to destroy and subvert
the glories of the universe that are us

we are more than we have imagined
more than we have invented and discovered
inside our pulsing dreams

sing with me of a better day
when we learn this planet as ourselves

we are this place shaping its tomorrows
we need to dream it well

genesis

"And the earth was without form, and void; and darkness was upon the face of the deep."
GENESIS 1:2 (KING JAMES VERSION)

I.

dark matter tendrils wove
a cosmic womb
bulging with amniotic fluids

dense and searing
blinding blue heat
spread across the blackness

imploding
exploding
birthing a shockwave
of hurled energy
a scatter of star seeds

glistening prisms
these stars were midwives
to our universe
iron to salt
water to copper
a rush of green
the blood of us

2.

the shards of our sun's placenta
formed our planet
her solar breath gusts
an umbilical cord of energy
that we ceaselessly feed upon

3.

this age of stars
is one short breath
in the universe's time
that will one day give way
to another age of darkness
where we are not even a memory

a note on the text

As a poet I tend to eschew traditional punctuation and, for the most part, forms. Thus, when organizing this book, I sought to stretch the ideas of the parts of speech with an ear towards poetical nuance contained in each word's paradigm. The section titled Nouns is the most traditionally defined, centering the book around people and place with time as a concept/thing. Prepositions is meant to investigate ideas of relationships to time, place, people. Interjections consists of compositions of reaction and feeling. Pronouns comprises poems of interrogation and reflection. And Conjunctions is more astral, focusing on places where two (or more) ideas, beings, and/or universal aspects meet and then pass by each other, continuing on their cyclical journeys.

acknowledgments

The following poems first appeared in the places listed:

“word time”: Torch LiteraryArts.org 2022

“error in time 2”: *Light on the Walls of Light*, Jambu Press, 2022

“downpressers,” “city values,” “writing love”: *Black Fire This Time*, Willow Books/Aquarius Press, 2022

“we are this place”: *Maestrapeace: San Francisco’s Monumental Feminist Mural*, Heydey Books, 2019

“city scat”: *Huizache: The Magazine of Latino Literature*, Centro-victoria at the University of Houston, Fall 2015

“creation paradox”: *Paterson Literary Review #26*, Passaic Community College, 1997

“who shall inherit the earth”: published as “prognostication in translation” *Occupy SF: Poems from the Movement*, Jambu Press, 2012

“rise”: commissioned poem for First Voice Show *Songs of J-Town*, 2022

PHOTO © MARK SHIGENAGA

about the author

Born and raised in California, granddaughter of immigrants, documented and undocumented, devorah major served as San Francisco's third Poet Laureate (2002–2006). Her poetry has carried her to many countries, where she has performed with and without musicians. In 2022 she received the Regina Coppola International Literary Award in Italy, where her sixth book of poetry, *with open arms*, was released in a bilingual edition in 2020. Her seventh book of poetry, *Califia's Daughter*, was published by Willow Press in 2020. major is featured on a number of CDs, including *Fierce//Love* and *The Tongue Is a Drum*, as a member of Daughters of Yam, a poetry and jazz performance duo with Opal Palmer Adisa. She has performed as poet and actress with First Voice productions of *Song of the City* in 2022 and *Soul of the City* in 2023 and 2024. She wrote the book for *Trade Routes*, a symphony by Guillermo Galindo that premiered under Maestro Michael Morgan and the Oakland East Bay Symphony in 2006. In June 2015, major premiered her poetry play *Classic Black: Voices of 19th-Century African Americans in San Francisco* at the San Francisco International Arts Festival.

devorah major flourishes with cross-genre interactions and has had productive creative collaborations with musicians, composers, painters, storytellers, and writers. She is always looking to build a better world and uses her science fiction stories as one voice in Afro-Futurism. She will put down her pen to march and call for justice. devorah major currently lives in Oakland.